Prince Edward Island

Rennay Craats

WEIGL EDUCATIONAL PUBLISHERS

Published by Weigl Educational Publishers Limited
6325 10 Street SE
Calgary, Alberta, Canada
T2H 2Z9
Web site: www.weigl.com

We acknowledge the financial support of the Government of Canada through the Book Publishing
Industry Development Program (BPIDP) for our publishing activities.

National Library of Canada Cataloguing in Publication Data
Craats, Rennay, 1973-
  Prince Edward Island / Rennay Craats.
  (Canadian sites and symbols)
  Includes index.
  ISBN 1-55388-030-7
  1. Provincial emblems--Prince Edward Island--Juvenile literature.
2. Heraldry--Prince Edward Island--Juvenile literature. I. Title.
II. Series.
CR213.P75C72 2003   j929.6'09717   C2003-910537-7

Printed in the United States of America
1 2 3 4 5 6 7 8 9 0   07 06 05 04 03

Project Coordinator: Donald Wells
Design: Janine Vangool
Layout: Virginia Boulay
Copy Editor: Tina Schwartzenberger
Photo Researchers: Barbara Hoffman
                         Pamela Wilton

Photograph Credits
Every reasonable effort has been made to trace ownership and to obtain permission to reprint
copyright material. The publishers would be pleased to have any errors or omissions brought to
their attention so that they may be corrected in subsequent printings.

Cover: Anne of Green Gables (**Barrett & MacKay**); **Barrett & MacKay:** pages 5, 7, 11, 15, 16, 17T, 17B, 20,
21T, 21B, 22; **Corel Corporation:** pages 3T, 3M, 3B, 4, 12, 13B, 14; **Government of PEI Executive Council:**
pages 1, 8, 19; **Ray Joubert:** page 10; **National Archives of Canada:** pages 6 (C0005796), 6R (insert)
(C-121336); **Parks Canada/Barrett & MacKay:** page 23; **Photos.com:** pages 9, 13T, 18.

Contents

Introduction

Canada is a large country. The ten Canadian provinces and three territories cover a vast amount of land. From one province or territory to another, the people, lifestyles, land, and animals are quite different. Each province and territory has its own **identity**. The provinces and territories use **symbols** to represent this identity. This book looks at the symbols that represent the province of Prince Edward Island.

Yukon Territory

Northwest Territories

Nunavut

British Columbia

Alberta

Manitoba

Saskatchewan

Fine white beaches cover the northern side of Prince Edward Island.

Prince Edward Island is Canada's smallest province. The island is located on the east coast of Canada. It is one of the maritime provinces, along with New Brunswick and Nova Scotia. The maritime provinces are also part of the Atlantic provinces, which include Newfoundland and Labrador. Prince Edward Island, or PEI, has a rich history and a promising future. The symbols of this province represent its **heritage**.

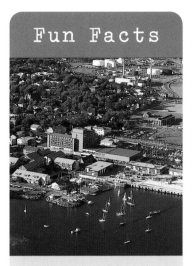

Fun Facts

Charlottetown is the capital of PEI. It is the province's largest city.

About 140,000 people live on PEI.

PEI covers about 5,660 square kilometres (2,185 square miles). It is about 230 kilometres (143 miles) long and from 6 to 60 kilometres (3.7 to 37 miles) wide.

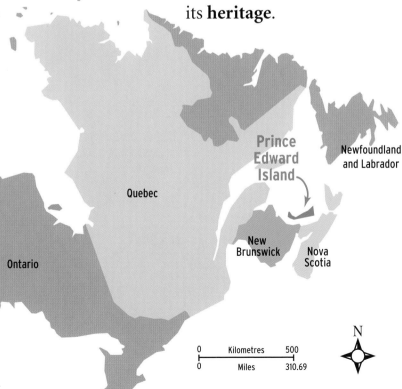

Ontario

Quebec

Prince Edward Island

Newfoundland and Labrador

New Brunswick

Nova Scotia

```
0        Kilometres      500
0          Miles       310.69
```

N

What's in a Name?

For such a small province, Prince Edward Island has a long name. It has been called by different names in the past. In 1603, it was called Île Saint-Jean after France claimed the island. When Great Britain took control of the area in 1763, it changed the name to Saint John's Island. In 1799, the British changed the name again. The name given to the province honoured Prince Edward Augustus, the Duke of Kent and Strathern. Prince Edward was the fourth son of Great Britain's King George III.

Charlottetown was named after Prince Edward's mother, Charlotte, wife of King George III.

While the province is officially named Prince Edward Island, it has many nicknames. PEI is called "the Garden Province" and "the Garden of the Gulf" because of the island's rich soil. The province is also called "the million-acre farm" because three-quarters of the island was once farmland. People who live on PEI call it "spud island" because it is well known for its potato crop. To most people on PEI, it is simply known as "the Island."

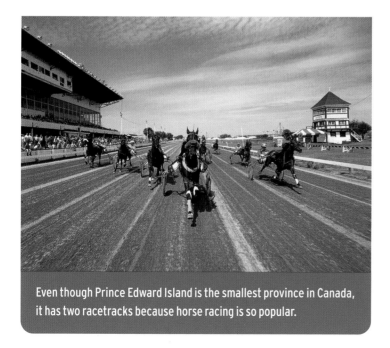

Even though Prince Edward Island is the smallest province in Canada, it has two racetracks because horse racing is so popular.

Fun Facts

The Mi'kmaq people called Prince Edward Island *Abegweit*, which means "cradled on the waves."

Saint John's Island is the English translation of Île Saint-Jean.

Prince Edward Island is often called the "Cradle of **Confederation**." In 1864, Charlottetown hosted the conference that led to Confederation.

There are two Prince Edward Islands. One is located in Canada. Another one is located in the southern Indian Ocean near South Africa.

Coat of Arms Closeup

Acoat of arms is a special design that represents a group or region. Each Canadian province and territory has its own coat of arms. Prince Edward Island's coat of arms is linked to its past as a British colony. Each part of the design symbolizes something special about the province.

Fun Facts

King Edward VII gave PEI its coat of arms on May 30, 1905. The design changed in 2002.

Many families on Prince Edward Island have their own coats of arms.

Features

A bluejay sits on top of the helmet. The bluejay is the official bird of Prince Edward Island.

Silver fox

The golden helmet on top of the shield represents the important role the province has played in Confederation.

Silver foxes on either side of the shield represent the hard-working, clever people of PEI.

A lion, a symbol of Great Britain, is on the top part of the shield.

The bottom of the shield displays a tall oak tree and three oak **saplings**. The saplings represent the three counties of Prince Edward Island—Kings county, Queens county, and Prince county. The oak tree represents Great Britain.

Lady slippers surround an eight-point star. They represent early European settlers. The eight-point star is a symbol used by the Mi'kmaq people to represent the Sun.

PEI's motto *Parva sub Ingenti*, Latin for "The Small Under the Protection of the Great," is at the bottom of the coat of arms.

Flying the Flag

Prince Edward Island's flag became official on March 24, 1964. The flag was created as part of celebrations to mark the 100th anniversary of the Charlottetown Conference. This conference led to the creation of Canada. The shield on the coat of arms was used to create the provincial flag. PEI did not have a provincial flag before 1964.

Like the official shield, the top of Prince Edward Island's flag has a lion on a red background, which stands for Great Britain. The oak tree and saplings sit on a white background on the bottom of the flag. The top, bottom, and right side of the flag have rectangular bands of red and white, Canada's official colours.

Fun Facts

PEI has an official **tartan** that was designed in 1960. The tartan colours are reddish-brown, green, white, and yellow. The reddish-brown colour represents PEI's red soil. Green symbolizes grass and trees. White stands for the white tops on waves in the ocean. Yellow stands for the Sun.

Prince Edward Island's Province House was built in 1847. This building is still used to house the provincial legislature.

Baby Seals and Bluejays

Bears, bobcats, caribou, cougars, and moose once lived on Prince Edward Island. Today, the largest wild land animals in the area are beavers, foxes, hares, raccoons, and skunks. Animals fill the waters surrounding PEI. Baby seals drift on floating sheets of ice each spring. Dolphins and different types of whales swim near the island. Sea life is abundant in the area. Clams, lobsters, mackerel, mussels, oysters, salmon, and trout are only a few of the sea creatures living around PEI. Although PEI has many types of animals, the province does not have an official animal symbol.

Visitors to Prince Edward Island often take a boat trip to see seals up close.

More than 300 types of birds can be found on Prince Edward Island during the spring, summer, and fall. Many of these birds stop to rest as they migrate north and south. Barred owls, black-capped chickadees, bluejays, crows, and ruffed grouse can be found in the area year-round. The marshes and bays of Prince Edward Island attract birds such as black and ring-necked ducks and the Canada goose.

Fun Facts

PEI is known for its lobsters. At one time, there were so many lobsters they were used as fertilizer.

Sometimes whales and dolphins swim into shallow water. They cannot return to deeper seas, and they become stranded on PEI's beaches. A group of trained volunteers called the PEI Stranding Network helps these animals get back to sea.

The bluejay was chosen to be the official bird of Prince Edward Island in a province-wide public vote in 1976.

Lady Slippers and Disappearing Trees

Rich, red soil makes it easy for different types of plants to grow on Prince Edward Island. Chokecherry, Queen Anne's lace, raspberry, tansy, and wild rose are common around the province. Blueberries, cranberries, and bayberry plants grow along the island's shores. In spring, wildflowers, including daisies, goldenrods, mayflowers, primroses, and violets, sprout from the ground. The province's official flower is the lady slipper. This type of orchid blooms in Prince Edward Island's wooded areas.

It is illegal to pick lady slippers on Prince Edward Island.

At one time, trees such as oak and white pine covered Prince Edward Island. In the 1800s, Great Britain used the area as a shipyard and cut down nearly all the beech, oak, and white pine trees for wood. Trees were also chopped down to make room for farms. Today, there are few original forests remaining on PEI. **Coniferous** trees are found in about 42 percent of the province. There are also balsam fir, birch, and red maple trees. The Prince Edward Island National Park was created to preserve some of PEI's remaining forests.

The red oak became the official tree of Prince Edward Island in 1987.

Fun Facts

Early settlers used red oak to make furniture and barrels because it is strong and heavy.

Beech and white pine trees have disappeared from PEI.

Mosses and different types of grasses grow in parts of PEI.

PEI has a rich soil that is ideal for growing crops. Unfortunately, some of the land has been farmed too much, and the soil lacks nutrients. Farmers have tried to plant different crops or have stopped planting in some areas to improve the soil.

Emblems of the Earth

Prince Edward Island was shaped thousands of years ago by **glaciers**. The glaciers slowly melted and pushed on the rock and soil beneath them. The pressure turned the rock and soil into sandstone. Iron oxide from this ancient sandstone has turned the province's soil red. The bright red sandstone and soil, the green plants and grasses, and the crystal blue water have come to represent Prince Edward Island.

There are no mines on Prince Edward Island, but it does produce gravel, peat, and sand. PEI has no official gemstone or mineral.

Prince Edward Island's red soil is ideal for growing potatoes. Potatoes are the primary source of income for the province's farms.

Prince Edward Island is well known for its gently rolling hills, colourful sandstone, and beautiful beaches. The province's coasts are also famous emblems of PEI. Years of wind and waves crashing against the shore have created high, red sandstone cliffs. The cliffs have become tourist attractions. Sand dunes block many of the inlets along the northern coastline. The coast has white, tan, pink, and red sands. The most important natural resource on Prince Edward Island is its rich, red soil. The Charlottetown soil was made the official soil of Prince Edward Island in 1997.

Fun Facts

Prince Edward Island's coastline is about 1,770 kilometres (1,100 miles) long.

Prince Edward Island receives an average of 3.4 metres (11.2 feet) of snow each year.

There are no mountains on Prince Edward Island. The highest point in the province is Springton in Queens County. The land in this area is 142 metres (466 feet) high.

Visitors come from all over the world to see PEI's beaches and cliffs.

A Seal of Approval

An official government seal is used to show that a government supports an important document, such as a treaty with another country or an act of parliament. Seals were originally dipped in melted wax and stamped onto a document. Today, governments use "impress" seals. A document is sealed by pressing it between two **engraved** plates. Prince Edward Island received its first seal from Great Britain in 1769. The design of the seal has changed during PEI's history. The seal was redesigned in 2002.

Seals were originally dipped in wax and stamped onto a document.

Features

The seals honouring British monarchs were replaced by the first provincial seal in 1949. In 1984, the government created a new seal that included Canada in the **inscription**. When the coat of arms was changed in 2002, the government decided to change the seal as well. The new seal was introduced on December 13, 2002. It displays the coat of arms in the centre of the circle. The top arc reads "Great Seal • Prince Edward Island • Canada." The French translation of this appears along the bottom of the seal.

The original 1769 seal contained the titles of George III. The other side of the seal showed an island base with a large oak tree on the right. A smaller oak tree with its trunk split into three trunks appeared on the left. The province's motto *Parva sub Ingenti* appeared below. Another Latin phrase, which means "Seal of the Island of St. John in America," surrounded this design.

Fun Facts

People have been sealing documents for hundreds of years. Seals were first used to visually prove to people who could not read that a document was authorized and issued by the proper person.

Special Places

Every province and territory has at least one special place that represents its heritage. Prince Edward Island has many such sites. One special place is the Prince Edward Island National Park. This 40-kilometre (25-mile) stretch of land has beaches, cliffs, grass-covered sand dunes, marshes, and small forests. The Prince Edward Island National Park is the home of Green Gables, the setting for Lucy Maud Montgomery's *Anne of Green Gables* books. The red-haired, **fictional** character, Anne, represents Prince Edward Island for many readers around the world. This small national park attracts thousands of people during the summer months.

The Green Gables House was built in the 1830s by relatives of Lucy Maud Montgomery.

Other special places in the province celebrate the people of the island. The Basin Head Fisheries Museum's exhibits show the life of an inshore **fisher** and how this life has changed over time. Exhibits and models show different fishing methods and materials. There is even an aquarium filled with saltwater fish. This museum is part of the PEI Museum and Heritage Foundation. Other heritage sites on Prince Edward Island include the Elmira Railway Station, the Fanning School, and the Orwell Corner Historic Village.

Fun Facts

Each year, the Charlottetown Festival presents the *Anne of Green Gables* musical play. More than 2 million people have watched Lucy Maud Montgomery's book come alive on stage since 1965. It is the longest running musical play in Canada.

Eastern Kings county is known for its singing sand beaches. The sand on these beaches makes a sharp sound when it is stepped on.

Confederation Bridge is 12.9 kilometres (8 miles) long and links Borden-Carleton, PEI, to Cape Tormentine, New Brunswick. It takes a vehicle about 12 minutes to cross the bridge.

Quiz

Based on what you have read, see if you can answer the following questions:

1. What is the capital of Prince Edward Island?

2. What are two of the province's nicknames?

3. What three animals appear on PEI's coat of arms?

4. In what year did PEI's provincial flag become official?

Beaconsfield Historic House was once the home of a wealthy shipbuilder. Today, it is open to the public for tours and special events.

5. True or false: PEI is home to bears, cougars, and moose.

6. What is the official flower of Prince Edward Island?

7. What is the colour of Prince Edward Island's soil?

8. What natural attractions can be found in Prince Edward Island National Park?

There is evidence that the ancestors of the Mi'kmaq people lived on Prince Edward Island 10,000 years ago. They were hunters and fishers.

Answers

8. Beaches, cliffs, grass-covered sand dunes, marshes, and forests

7. Red

6. The lady slipper

5. False

4. 1964

3. A bluejay, a lion, and silver foxes

2. "The Garden Province," "Garden of the Gulf," "Million-acre farm," "Spud Island," or "the Island"

1. Charlottetown

Glossary

Confederation: the joining of the Canadian provinces to form one country

coniferous: trees that have cones and needles

engraved: cut or carved into a hard surface

fictional: not real; invented

fisher: people who fish for food or sport

glaciers: slow-moving rivers of ice

heritage: something handed down from earlier generations

identity: the qualities that make one person or thing different from all others

inscription: words written or carved onto something

saplings: young trees

symbols: things that stand for something else

tartan: colourful striped pattern that often represents a group of people

Index